Editor
Cathy S. Gilbert, M.S. Ed.

Editorial Project Manager
Ina Massler Levin, M.A.

Editor in Chief
Sharon Coan, M.S. Ed.

Illustrator
Barb Lorseydi

Cover Artists
Sue Fullam
Jose L. Tapia

Associate Designer
Denise Bauer

Creative Director
Elayne Roberts

Imaging
James Edward Grace
Ralph Olmedo, Jr.

Product Manager
Phil Garcia

Acknowledgements:
HyperStudio® is a registered trademark of Roger Wagner Publishing

Publishers:
Rachelle Cracchiolo, M.S. Ed.
Mary Dupuy Smith, M.S. Ed.

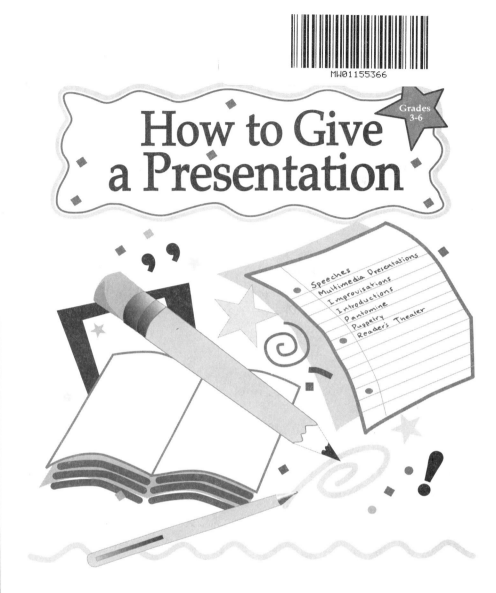

How to Give a Presentation

Grades 3-6

Speeches
Multimedia Presentations
Improvisations
Introductions
Pantomime
Puppetry
Reader's Theater

Author:

Kathleen Christopher Null

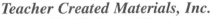

Teacher Created Materials

Teacher Created Materials, Inc.
6421 Industry Way
Westminster, CA 92683
www.teachercreated.com

ISBN-1-57690-325-7

©*1997 Teacher Created Materials, Inc.*

Reprinted, 1999

Made in U.S.A.

Table of Contents

Introduction

How to Give a Presentation offers you a series of speaking and listening activities to introduce your students to a variety of ways to prepare and present material to a group. Divided into several sections, the book takes your students through the various steps necessary to prepare and organize presentations.

The book is divided in the following way:

- **Organizing and Preparing Presentations**

  Students will be given the tools to get organized and to help prepare presentations.

- **Let Me Introduce**

  Students will begin to find out more about themselves so they can present themselves to their classmates and others.

- **Improvisation**

  Students will participate in various activities that will help them to "think on their feet."

- **With a Dramatic Flair**

  Students will have the opportunity to explore their dramatic presentation skills.

- **Lights, Camera, Action!**

  Students will write, perform, and produce different dramatic presentations, refining those from the previous sections.

- **Make a Joyful Noise!**

  Students will take part in noisy, exuberant activities that will lead to better presentations.

- **Tech Talk**

  Students will be introduced to various forms of multimedia that will allow them to enhance presentations that they give.

Use this book as a springboard for enriching oral language learning. You may want to combine some of the methods presented to create new activities and add additional material of your own. Be creative and have fun with these materials. Soon your students will say with enthusiasm and confidence, "I can give a presentation."

Prewriting Plans

Prewriting is a way to plan ahead. It is a good idea to organize before you create a presentation. When you take the time to write all your ideas before creating your presentation, it will be easier to put together the completed project quickly. The most important thing about prewriting is that it is like a blueprint for your project. A blueprint is a plan for building a house. No one would ever build a house without one. If you tried, you'd end up with a messy pile of lumber, and you would have wasted lots of time and money. But if you make a blueprint first, you'll know exactly how the house will look and what you'll need to do to build it. Here are some prewriting plans to try.

Brainstorming

One of the first and most enjoyable tools to use as you plan most of your projects is brainstorming. You can brainstorm by yourself, but if you can do it with another person or a group, you'll generate more ideas. To brainstorm, all you need is something to write on, something to write with, and your brain. Begin by writing down every idea that comes to you, no matter what. Don't judge any of your ideas. Watch out! If you find yourself saying or thinking "That was a stupid idea!" or "Where did that idea come from!" you'll know you're judging. If you start doing that, take a deep breath and keep the ideas coming. Some thoughts will seem unimportant, but write them down anyway because they just might lead to other really great ideas. You may brainstorm a title idea, a list of questions or topics, a problem, a plot, a character, or anything you want. When you think you've run out of ideas, take a deep breath and keep writing. Sometimes the flow of ideas slows and then speeds again. When you're sure you have no more ideas or you're sure you have enough that you like, then you can look more carefully at your list and pick the best ones.

Example of a brainstorming list for a poem about nature:

- nature
- nice
- stormy
- dark
- clouds
- rainy
- thunder
- scary

- splashing
- puddles
- boots
- tight boots
- blisters
- pain
- cold
- runny nose

- hot soup
- bright red raincoat
- clouds blowing away
- wet windows
- blue sky
- white clouds
- green grass
- thirsty

Here is the poem a student wrote after brainstorming. Notice that not every idea listed is used.

The sound of rain calls me outside
to splash in the puddles,
but my boots are tight and the sky is dark;
I am cold and my nose runs.
My mom gives me soup, and I look at my red raincoat
hanging by the window, and there's blue sky;
I see out the window the clouds are leaving
and taking the puddles with them.
"Hey!" I say, "I wasn't finished yet!"

Prewriting Plans (cont.)

Webs and Clusters

Webs and clusters are another form of brainstorming, but instead of just listing ideas, you place them on your paper in relation to each other with lines connecting ideas. You may begin with a topic or phrase and create a web or cluster that branches off the topic "nucleus" circled in the center of the cluster.

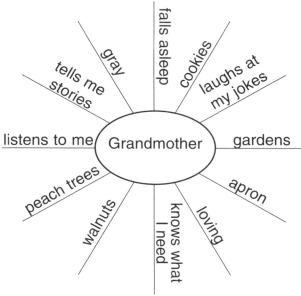

Choose a topic of interest to you and use the blank cluster below to record your brainstorming ideas for your topic. Put the main topic in the center of the cluster.

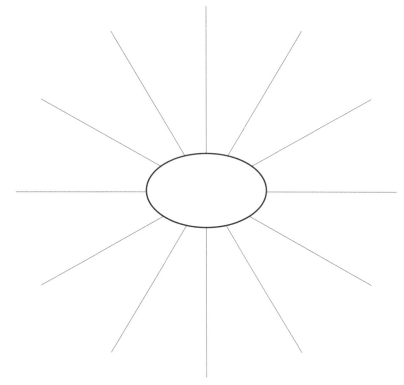

Prewriting Plans *(cont.)*

Outlines

Many writers prefer to begin with an outline. To outline, choose two or more main ideas and assign them Roman numerals: I., II., III., etc. Next, divide each main idea into subtopics and give each of these its own line and letter: A., B., C., etc. These subtopics may require their own divisions; if so, they are assigned Arabic numbers: 1., 2., 3., etc. And if these need further division, they will be labled with lowercase letters: a., b., c., etc.

Outline

I. Topic introduction

II. Main Body

   A. First Subtopic

     1. Description of the subtopic

     2. Further information on the subtopic

       a. a detail about the information in 2

       b. another detail about the information in 2

   B. Second Subtopic

     1. Description of the second subtopic

     2. More information about the second subtopic

   C. Third Subtopic

     1. Description of the third subtopic

       a. a detail about the description

       b. another detail

     2. More information about the third subtopic

III. Conclusion

   A. Summary of subtopics

   B. Concluding remark

Here is an example of an outline for the topic of "Fads"

I. Introduction

   A. Fifties fads

   B. Sixties fads

II. Fifties Fads

   A. Slinkies

     1. What they look like

     2. How they were invented

       a. About the inventor

       b. Problems inventor encountered

     3. How they gained popularity

   B. Hula Hoops

     1. All about their invention

     2. Amateur Hula Hooping

       a. How to spin the hoop

       b. Games

     3. Competitive Hula Hooping

III. Sixties Fads

   A. Beatles

     1. Their origins

       a. "The Cavern"

       b. Liverpool

     2. Their first tour of America

     3. Their music

   B. Fashions

     1. The mini-skirt

     2. Go-go boots

     3. Granny dresses

   C. Hippies

     1. Clothing and hairstyles

     2. Lifestyle

IV. Conclusion

   A. Fifties Summary

   B. Sixties Summary

Prewriting Plans *(cont.)*

Storyboards

Storyboards help you plan a presentation that will use both visual aids (objects, actions, pictures, videos, slides) and sound (music, sounds, speaking). You can use this storyboard form or create your own.

Text Notes	Visual	Audio

Making Changes

Proofreading

When you first write or plan a presentation, you should feel free to be creative. Don't worry if spelling is correct, or even if your ideas are good enough. Just keep writing and planning. Think of this stage as being another form of brainstorming. Once you have all your ideas on paper, you can check to see if you made any sense. Go over your work two or three times and check for spelling and grammar errors. Be sure to read out loud what you've written. You'll find more things that need to be changed. It is always a good idea to have others check your work, too.

Editing

At the editing stage you should still be alert to spelling and grammar errors, but you will now focus even more on the content. Did you say what you wanted to say? Are you clear? Read your work or try a presentation in front of others to make sure your meaning is clear. You can write all over your rough draft or plan. Circle words or phrases that you want to check. Cross out anything that does not work. Draw arrows to show where to move a phrase that would work better somewhere else. Don't worry about crossing out part of your work. You will continue to get good ideas. If you are not sure about eliminating part of your work, copy it someplace else so you can keep it in a file. You might change your mind or use it for some other presentation. After you have done the first editing, it is a good idea to set your work aside for the rest of the day or the rest of the week if you have time. Then when you're ready to revise the work, you will have a fresh outlook.

Revising

Now it is time to revise your work. It may be that all you have to do is rewrite using all the notes, additions, and scribbles that appear on the first draft. As you work, you may have more ideas for making your presentation even better. That's okay. Editing and revising are sometimes an ongoing process that keeps recycling until you are pleased with your work. Don't worry if you are still not satisfied with your final written presentation. If there is time, you can repeat any or all of the steps above. Even then, don't be surprised if you turn in your best work and a day or a week later see all the things you would change about it if you could. Even the most famous artists and writers usually feel the same way. Creating is a process that never ends. With each project you do, you learn more about how to make the next one even better.

Introduction

Students of all ages dread that first day of class when the teacher asks them to tell the class something about themselves. Being unprepared might be a portion of the dread. Certainly one feels a bit more confident when one has something to say. On page 10, you will find a student profile, *This Is Me!* Students will enjoy filling in information about themselves. When it is time for the students to introduce themselves to the class, they will be prepared and know just what to say. Shyer or younger students may simply read their responses, or they may stand while someone else reads about them. Another way to make the introductions would be to go over each response one at a time as a whole class. You could ask, "How many have brown eyes?" for a whole class response, for instance. Afterwards, you may wish to keep the profiles in a file for your own use. You will find an activity titled, *More About Me!* (pages 11–12) which includes tips for giving speeches, including how to deal with the everpresent stage fright and a plan for writing and giving an autobiographical speech. *Let Me Show You!* (pages 13–14) is a show-and-tell activity which includes pointers on how to follow directions. This activity contains a quick and fun quiz to find out how many students have learned to follow directions. After that your students will never again take directions for granted. *Let Me Show You!* is a good activity to precede the show-and-tell activity, *Guess What!* in the Make a Joyful Noise section (page 37).

Who Hates Pizza?, an ice-breaking game found on page 15, will enable students to get to know their classmates. This will be helpful for the activity following, *Reporting Live!* (page 16). Students will need to search for the unique in order to interview their classmates. With the biographical speech activity, *Allow Me to Introduce . . .* on page 17, students will build upon what they learned in preparing their autobiographical speeches. You may have students choose someone they know, someone in the community or a fictional character to profile. Or you may prefer to give students a list of historical figures from which to choose.

Students will get to experience modern technology with the video/biography activity, *The Life and Times of . . .* (page 18). Again, subjects may be real or fictional, contemporary or historical. You may prefer to have students do a biographical speech on a person who is historical and then choose a contemporary subject for the video/biography, or vice versa. You will need to judge the abilities of your students and challenge them accordingly. These activities not only teach your students to stand before others to present ideas but will also reinforce learning in such subjects as social studies, language arts, and science.

This Is Me!

Anyone can feel nervous on that first day of school when the teacher asks students to introduce themselves. You will feel more confident when you have prepared a presentation in advance.

Answer these questions about yourself. When you are finished, your teacher will ask you to share your answers with the class.

1. What is your full name? _____

2. Do you have a nickname? If so, do you wish to share it? _____
   _____

3. What does your family like to do together? _____
   _____

4. Do you have any pets? _____

5. Where did you go the last time you traveled? _____
   _____

6. What things do you like to do?_____
   _____

7. What is your favorite food? _____

8. What is your favorite color? _____

9. What color are your eyes? _____

10. What is your favorite sport to play? _____

11. What is your favorite sport to watch?_____

12. What is your favorite book, so far? _____

13. What do you like the most about school? _____
    _____

14. What do you dislike most about school? _____
    _____

15. If you could be any animal, what would you be and why? _____
    _____

16. Do you have brothers and sisters? If you do, tell their names and ages. _____
    _____

17. What do you dream of doing someday? _____
    _____
    _____

More About Me!

This is your opportunity to introduce yourself to your classmates in a 2–4 minute speech about you. But before we get to your speech, what about those butterflies flitting around in your stomach? Many, many people are afraid to give a speech. If you are one of them, you are not alone. The tips below will help.

What to Do About Stage Fright

1. First of all, remember that many people get some butterflies or nervous feelings when they need to stand in front of an audience. So remember that your nervousness is normal.

2. If you are really nervous, you can imagine that you are a famous actor or actress just playing a role. Imagine that everyone in the audience is really nervous and you are not nervous at all.

3. You might try choosing two or three friendly faces in the audience and give your speech to them. Just don't forget the rest of your audience.

How to Make Yourself Clear

1. Practice enough so that you need only a few notes.

2. If you need to look down at notes, be sure to lift your head up as much as possible so the audience can hear you clearly.

3. Don't speak as rapidly as you would to your best friend on the telephone. When you have several people listening, it takes a bit longer for your message to get across. Be sure each word is pronounced clearly and does not slide into the next word.

4. Don't speak so slowly that your audience falls into a hypnotic trance. Vary the rate.

5. Be sure you are loud enough. Perhaps your teacher will signal you if you are not loud enough.

How to Be a Hit

1. Don't be a robot speaker; be your usual animated self. It's okay to move around and use your hands. It's okay to make a joke or two related to your speech. Be careful not to move around too much, or your audience will become so focused on your moving that they'll forget to listen.

2. Avoid slang and unclear speech but speak as naturally as you can.

3. Rely on notes as little as possible and speak freely as much as possible. A good way to do this for a speech is to write key words only on your notecards and speak from those key words. For instance, you could just use the word "trip" to remind yourself to tell your audience about an embarrassing thing that happened to you the last time you were on a trip with your family.

More About Me! *(cont.)*

How to Be a Hit *(cont.)*

4. Instead of thinking of a speech as a form of cruel and unusual punishment, write a speech that you would enjoy giving. Watch your audience to see how they are reacting to the things you are saying. You might even find some ways to allow *them* to participate by asking them questions. For instance, you might say, "Last summer we camped in Kings Canyon. How many of you have been to Kings Canyon?"

Now, on with Your Speech!

◆ Begin by brainstorming a list of things about you that you want to include. Some topics might be hobbies, pets, sports, your family, where you're from, your best subjects, things you like to do in the summer, favorite foods, an embarrassing thing that happened to you, the best thing that ever happened, what you want to do in the future, or your pet peeves. Use the "This Is Me" form on page 10 to help you.

◆ Use your list to make an outline. From your outline, you can highlight the key ideas or put them on notecards. Follow the format below for the structure of your speech.

◆ You will need to practice. Time your speech to be sure that it is around two to four minutes long. Then practice some more. Practice in front of a mirror, in front of your dog, your parents, your friends, or a row of teddy bears. The more you practice, the more confident you will feel, and you will be able to concentrate on what you want to say instead of worrying so much about making a mistake.

Autobiographical Speech Format

I. **Introduction:** greet your audience and tell them your name.

II. **Attention getter:** share a joke about yourself, or begin with an interesting start that will get the attention of your audience. ("I'm going to tell you about the time I was left at the airport and my family accidentally flew home without me . . . ")

III. **Body of your speech:** include the main points of your speech here. (You shouldn't finish your airport story here; keep your audience in suspense. Tell everything about yourself here. Some of the things you say can lead to your airport story. For instance, if you got left behind at the airport because you were playing a game in the arcade, be sure to mention that you really, really love arcade games.)

IV **The most exciting part of your speech:** this is where you illustrate your main points with details. Think of this part as the dessert. Now you can tell your audience what happened to you.

V. **Conclusion:** summarize here. Bring your speech full circle. (You might mention here that you never play airport arcade games anymore. Or that your luggage was lost in another state and you're still waiting for it.)

VI. **Thank your audience.**

Let Me Show You!

Reading and following directions is an important skill to learn in order to prepare successful class presentations. Here are some pointers for following directions. After you have become an expert in following directions, see how well you do with the show-and-tell directions on the next page.

◆ Begin at the beginning. Often we are impatient and want to get started with something new, so we plunge in. The problem with jumping in is that we might miss an important direction, and we'll end up wishing we hadn't. If you are feeling as if you want to hurry, take a deep breath and slow down. Read or listen to the directions from the very beginning.

◆ Pay attention to the details. Again, if we are in a hurry, we might miss something important, or we might misunderstand the directions. There are many cooks in the world who, in a hurry, thought the recipe said one cup of salt when it really said one cup of sugar. Have you ever tasted salty cookies?

◆ Ask questions. If you do not understand a direction, ask your teacher, a parent, or a friend. Don't continue until you understand. Read or listen to all the directions before you begin. A very important direction might be saved for last.

◆ If, after you begin, you're not sure, go back to the directions. Sometimes they are more clear the second time you read them.

Fill in the following to see how well you can follow directions.

1. Read all the directions before you begin.

2. Write your middle name here: _____

3. Subtract your mother's birth year from your birth year and write the answer here: _____

4. Take the answer from #3 above and add your father's birth year. The total is _____

5. Write the date here: _____

6. Add all the numbers of the date and write the sum here: _____

7. Take the total from #6 and add it to the total of #4 above. _____

8. You do not need to do any of the above except for #1 and #9. _____

9. Write your name here if you followed all the directions correctly:

_____

I am good at following directions!

Let Me Show You! *(cont.)*

One of the best ways to introduce yourself to others is by showing them things that have a special meaning for you. Follow the directions below to prepare for your special show-and-tell presentation:

1. Read all these directions and ask your teacher if you do not understand any of them.
2. Take these directions home with you so you will know how to prepare.
3. Find these items to bring to class:
   a. An item to represent your family: something to represent your ethnic background, where your family comes from and your culture, what your family likes to do, or something to represent your family name. (See example below).
   b. A photograph that is special to you: your family, you as a baby, you playing a sport, or your grandparents. Be sure to check with a parent before bringing any photograph that might be valuable. You may need to make a copy of the photo to bring to class and leave the original at home.
   c. A food to represent you: your favorite food, a food that represents your family, or even a food you really dislike.
   d. A book to represent you: a favorite book, a book written by a family member, a book you've created, or a scrapbook.
   e. An item to represent you: a favorite piece of jewelry, a piece of sports equipment, a wooden box, a toy from when you were younger, a rock from your favorite camping place.

   f. Something you have made: a painting or drawing, a collage, a puppet, a sculpture, an article of clothing, something knitted, woodworking, leather-craft, or beads, for example.
4. Put each of your six chosen items together in a container and bring them to school on_____.
5. Be prepared to talk about each item.

Example:

Keisha brought a box of things to school to share. First, she showed her classmates a wooden sculpture from Africa. She explained that her family originally came from Africa and that the sculpture was from the same area her family came from. Next, she showed everyone a photograph of herself when she was a baby. Everyone said she was really cute. Then she pulled a copy of *Little Women* from her collections box. She said her mother just finished reading it to her and that it took a long time because her mother had kept crying. Keisha said that she plans to keep the book and read it to her children. Next she brought out a dress. She explained that her grandmother made it for her for Kwanzaa. Everyone said it was very colorful. Then she unrolled a tube to show a painting she made of a forest with lots of colorful birds. She explained that she had painted it after she got home from a vacation where they had fed the birds in the forest. She painted it so she could feel better about not being there anymore. She said she can look at the painting and feel as if she's there.

Who Hates Pizza?

Your teacher will tell you how much time you have to go about the room finding someone for each blank below. Remember, you can only use each name once, and the person who meets the requirement must sign his or her own name. You cannot call across the room and fill in the blanks yourself; you must speak to each person to see if he or she can sign any blanks.

Who has green eyes? _____

Who was born in another state? _____

Who was born in another country? _____

Who hates pizza? _____

Who likes broccoli? _____

Who has no sisters? _____

Who has no brothers? _____

Who has a parent in the military? _____

Who is an aunt or an uncle? _____

Who has an unusual name? _____

Who has an unusual pet? _____

Who plays on a sports team? _____

Who has acted on stage? _____

Who writes poetry? _____

Who has baked bread? _____

Who likes to snowboard?_____

Who has been rock climbing? _____

Who has more than one dog? _____

Who likes to sing? _____

Who plays a musical instrument? _____

Who has red hair? _____

Who loves to read? _____

Who has been white-water rafting? _____

Who has taken ballet? _____

Who speaks two or more languages? _____

Another game to break the ice: prepare "nametags" by writing the names of famous characters on them—e.g., "Peter Pan," "Charlie" (of the chocolate factory), or "Scrooge." Students wear the nametags on their backs and try to guess who they are by asking their classmates only yes or no questions.

Reporting Live!

Half the class will be assigned the roles of reporters. If you are a reporter, your job will be to interview a classmate in order to give your report. Take your notebook and pencil and brainstorm the best questions you can create. Interview your subject, take good notes, and report to the class. Later, you will trade roles and you will be interviewed. Here is a sample interview to give you an idea:

"This is Jason B. reporting live from Mrs. Hammond's class, room 22. I am here with Chris N., who has been so kind to grant me this interview. How are you, Chris?"

"Fine, thank you, good to be here."

"Chris, I have learned something about you that I think will be news to our audience and that is that you are a competitive motocross bicyclist. Is that true?"

"Yes, it is."

"So tell me—what is it like riding a bicycle through the mud and crashing?"

"Well, dirty. And I get bruised and scuffed up, but it's a lot of fun."

"How did you ever get started in this? Did you fall off your tricycle in the mud when you were three years old and decide that this was for you?"

"Basically, yes. Actually, I used to go ride in the fields by my house with my brother. I'd come home all muddy, and my mother would freak. But now I am earning prizes, so she's not freaking anymore."

"Really, so now she likes it?"

"Well, I'm not so sure about that, but she supports me."

"That's great. We'll get to some more interesting things about Chris after this. Back to you in the studio. This is Jason B. reporting live."

Your class may decide to videotape your interview and create an entire class television show featuring all the interviews and maybe a few commercials as well (see page 34), so hold on to those interview notes!

Do you need some help creating interview questions? Work together in groups of three to four students to list as many questions as you can think of to use in your interview. Write the questions on the back of this page to use later as you need them.

Allow Me to Introduce . . .

Some speakers think it is much easier to give a speech about another person than to give a speech introducing themselves. Perhaps you will agree. With the biographical speech you have many more choices, and that could be a plus. First of all, you can choose your subject. Your subject may be someone you know, someone from the community, or a fictional or historical figure. Next, you can choose whether to give a speech about your subject, or act as your subject and let him or her speak.

1. You will need to do some research and some prewriting. Collect as many facts as you can about your subject. To do this, go to the library to look in encyclopedias, magazines, or other references. A librarian will gladly help you find books on your subject. If the subject of your biographical speech is still living, ask the person as many questions as you can.

2. Organize your facts with an outline, notecards, and/or a web.

3. Now organize your speech. You may follow the rough outline below or create a more specific outline of your own.

   I. Opening words (get the attention of your listeners and let them know who and what your speech is about).

   II. Details (about your main points).

   III. Concluding remarks (summarizing and ending).

Remember to include the following in your speech:

- Name and identity of your subject

- Significance of your subject (what he or she does, who he or she is,

  what role he or she has played in a book or history)

- Something special about your subject

- The time in which he or she lived or now lives.

- A typical day for your subject

The Life and Times of . . .

This is your opportunity to make a video documentary or biography about someone important. You may choose someone you know—for example, your grandfather, the lady down the street who makes bowls and mugs on a potter's wheel in her garage, or the mayor of your town. Or you may create a video biography about a character in a book you have read. You may play the part of the character or have a friend dress up like the character and share his or her life on camera. You will want to write a script, so you will be sure to include all the important details about your character. (The storyboard on page 7 may be helpful.) Your teacher may ask you to create a documentary about someone you have studied in history or social studies. In that case, you will want to find some information from books and computer programs. You might want to act the role of the historical figure or write a script for a friend. See the biographical speech on page 17 for more ideas about what to include in your video biography.

If your subject is available, you can interview and videotape the person while he or she is engaged in some typical activities. If your subject is fictional, you can interview the actor and videotape him or her acting out a script of what might be typical activities. If your subject is historical, this is your chance to direct a period piece. You could direct Napoleon leading a battle or Martin Luther King, Jr., giving his famous "I Have a Dream" speech.

Don't forget to look for the unusual. Your documentary will be much more interesting if you can dig up truly interesting facts about your subject.

Though you will videotape longer, limit your presentation to three to five minutes. If you edit out the parts that are slower and less interesting, your documentary will be stronger.

Introduction

Often students who would feel uncomfortable about standing in front of the class "forget" to feel uncomfortable when distracted by a spontaneous improvisation. This section contains five such activities to inspire even the introverts to speak. First there is an activity (page 20) that will involve the entire class (and even utilize math skills). You may proceed with the activity as is, or you may enhance it with the following ideas:

1. Cut pictures from magazines to represent the items for "sale." The mounted pictures can be given to each buyer.

2. Cut pictures from magazines and catalogs of unusual or luxury items to "sell" (rhinestone studded sneakers, autographed Beatles poster, etc.).

3. Have students bring in toys, books, or other items that they no longer use and auction these items off.

Next is a tongue twister activity, *The Tongue Twister Show!* (page 21). Students write tongue twisters and then try them out on unsuspecting good sports. Your students may try them out on students in other classes or school staff. To extend this activity, have students videotape those who are attempting to recite the tongue twisters. Student teams could produce their own tongue twisters show by writing a script, planning the production (storyboard forms can be found on page 7), and then taking a video camera "on location" to the school grounds, the neighborhood, or their families. The results could be viewed in a class film festival.

Once students have twisted their tongues, impromptu speaking shouldn't be that formidable. The activity on page 22 contains several impromptu speaking prompts. They can be cut apart and kept in a box. To use them, have each student draw a prompt for on-the-spot speaking. You may decide to allow students to see their prompt five or ten minutes in advance, or you may prefer that each draw a prompt and begin his or her speech immediately, depending upon the abilities of your students. You may prefer to have students give their speeches on one day, or you may wish to have one or two students give impromptu speeches each day during a transition between subjects.

Story Telling with Oomph! (page 23) presents several ways to introduce storytelling forms that include drama. You may wish to use all of them in order or pick one that suits you and your students. These activities lead into the reader's theater activity (page 29).

You will find *Drama-on-the-Spot* (page 24) takes the concept of impromptu speaking a step further. In this activity, student teams of two or three draw a slip of paper from a box (or hat, or perhaps a box painted to look like a theater). Each student team gets a moment to discuss who will play which role and grab a prop or two. The scenarios on this page may also be used in other activities. Students may enjoy borrowing a scenario for the dialogue from *Dramatic Dialogue* (page 30) or the *Filmmaking* activity (page 32).

Auction!

Your teacher will auction the things on this list to the highest bidder. You have $100.00 in play money to spend at the auction. Bid for what you really want. Keep track of how much you spend and what you buy. When you wish to bid on an item, raise your hand, or your teacher may ask you to make a certain sound, say a certain word, or do something unusual to indicate you are bidding.

1. A trip to wherever you want to go (Tell the class where if you win.)

2. All the clothes you want

3. Good friends for the rest of your life

4. Straight A's

5. Any pet you want (If you win, say what kind you want.)

6. Your dream job (If you win, say what it is.)

7. To be a famous athlete (In what sport?)

8. To never be sick again

9. A huge collection of coins or stamps (State which and why.)

10. To be a TV or movie star

11. A happy family

12. All the books you want

13. To be a famous artist

14. To speak another language (State which and why.)

15. To be a musician (What kind?)

16. A shopping spree at your favorite store (State which and why.)

17. To be trained as an astronaut

18. To sail around the world

19. All the latest computer equipment

20. To be in a parade (Doing what?)

The Tongue Twisters Show!

Everyone gets his or her tongue tangled from time to time. Sometimes it happens when we don't want it to. In this activity you will be twisting your own tongue and the tongue of others on purpose. Begin by saying "toy boat" quickly five times. How did you do? Next try some of these:

> What a shame such a shapely sash should such shabby stitches show.

> Billy Button bought a buttered biscuit; did Billy Button buy a buttered biscuit? If Billy Button bought a buttered biscuit, where's the buttered biscuit Billy Button bought?

> I'd rather be rooked by crooked crooks than choke on crumbly cookies baked by ruthless cooks too lazy to look at cookbooks.

> The sixth sheik's sixth sheep's sick.

> Betty Botter's batter is better than her brother's bitter batter because she bought a better butter.

> She sells seashells by the seashore. The shells she sells are surely seashells. So if she sells shells on the seashore, I'm sure she sells seashore shells.

Now try some of your own. When you have a few in addition to the ones listed above, take your favorite ones and try them out on others. Write them clearly so that they are easy to read. Your teacher will have your tongue twisters tested (that's a tongue twister!) in front of the whole class. You may try them on people outside the class and create a "Tongue Twisters Show" by videotaping people attempting to say your tongue twisters.

_____

_____

_____

_____

_____

_____

_____

_____

Impromptu Speaking

An impromptu speech is one that has not been prepared or rehearsed. These presentations will not be polished, perfect speeches. Have fun with them and use your imagination. (Cut the following list apart and have each student draw a topic.)

Why Grass Is Green	What Makes Me Really Mad
Elephants	What I Think About Aliens
What Makes People Laugh	If I Could Invent a Candy
The Best Pet to Have	Why Dogs Are Better Than Cats (or vice versa)
My History of Bicycles	Why It's Important to Read
How I Feel About Television	The Best Way to Get Exercise
My Favorite Kind of Music	My Favorite Movie
The First Time I Ever Cooked	What I Dislike About School
What I Like About school	Which Is a Better Place to Live, the Mountains or the Beach?
My Favorite Day of the Year	How to Make Lots of Money
How to Shop for a Gift	The Best Kind of Car to Drive
Marshmallows	How to Promote World Peace
My Favorite Pair of Shoes	The Best Things About Summer
A Person I Admire	What I Don't Like About Birthdays

Storytelling with Oomph!

This page will inspire you to use storytelling as a dramatic form.

1. Choose an appropriate story for your students. Be sure it has characters and interesting events. Practice reading it aloud with your own interpretations. Add emotion, create voices for the characters, and find ways to emphasize action and suspense with your voice and body language. For example, lean forward and whisper for suspense, use a hurried, excited voice for quickly moving action, and exaggerate different voices for the different characters. Read the story to your students to introduce them to the rest of the activities.

2. Have your students choose stories to prepare for presentation. Tell them to be sure to practice at home before their "performance" time.

3. Assign various students to make a noise for various forms of punctuation in a story that you will read aloud. They should each have a copy of the story, or you can point to each student when his or her punctuation mark comes up. For example, a student might clap for a period, another might snap his fingers for a comma, another might make a funny mouth noise for quotation marks, and another might jump up and say "hooray" for an exclamation mark.

4. Choose a story with many characters. As a class, or in groups, read the story together. Assign roles to the students. Students will read the quotations of their characters. Have another student read the narration. Instruct them to put feeling into their roles.

5. Assign each student an emotion such as disgust, love, joy, sadness, fear, excitement, loneliness, anger. Give them the following list of words and have each student read the list with the emotion he or she has been assigned.

• hello	• spinach
• good-bye	• rain
• ice cream	• school
• homework	• weeds
• money	• sport cars
• friends	• television
• roller coaster	• darkness

6. Have students choose stories to read into a tape recorder. Tell them to add emotion, varied voices, and sound effects. Have a "radio day" and play the recordings for the class.

Drama-on-the-Spot

Cut these scenarios apart. Students may draw them at random and create two-and three-character dramas. Set a timer for each dramatization so they do not go over three to five minutes.

Character #1 was driving too fast. Character #2 is a police officer.

Character #1 has just hit a baseball through character #2's window.

Character #1 wants to use the telephone to tell his or her mom that he or she will be late. Character #2 is having a long chat with a friend.

Character #1 just found out that he or she will be moving. Character #2 is upset. Character #3 is glad.

Characters #1 and #2 are having an argument. Character #3 wants to end it nicely.

Characters #1 is trying to sell an old bicycle to character #2.

Character #1 and #2 go to the pet store to buy their first dog from character #3.

Character #1 is trying to read a book but character #2 wants to play.

Character #1 is babysitting character #2 who is very active and curious.

Characters #1, 2, and 3 have just gotten into a fender bender with each other.

Character #1 has just spent hours cooking a special meal for character #2. The meal is horrible.

Character #1 has lost his or her voice and is trying to explain to character #2 why he or she can't go out.

Character #1 is trying to return an article of clothing that fell apart in the washing machine. Character #2 is the store clerk.

Character #1 has just sprained his or her ankle on a city sidewalk. Characters #2 and 3 are passersby.

Character #1 is visiting from another country and doesn't speak the language. He or she tries to tell characters #2 and 3 that she or he really needs to find a restroom!

Character #1 (in a fancy restaurant) is just about to ask character #2 a very important question when the waiter, character #3, drops a tray of food.

Character #1 is a schoolteacher and characters #2 and 3 are friendly students who've just come into class with poison oak rashes.

Character #1 has just crushed the fender of the car of character #2 who happens to be the school principal.

Character #1 and character #2 have just shown up at character #3's party, and they are dressed alike.

Introduction

Although all civilizations have some form of dramatic presentations today, no one knows precisely where or when drama first started. One theory about origins suggests that a natural love of storytelling led inevitably to a growing recognition of those people talented in expression of feelings and recreation of actions. This in turn led to greater appreciation by audiences and wider currency of dramatic stories until eventually drama itself comprised a central—in some societies, perhaps crowning— position of cultural identity. Through the ages, a core repository of classic dramatic forms and repertory have become the heritage of the world, crossing national, cultural, and racial boundaries. The basic content types are generally classified as tragedy, serious drama, melodrama, and comedy. All cultures seem to have produced most of these types, albeit in different forms or formats.

One of the earliest forms of drama which is still popular is puppetry. An experience in *Puppetry* can be found on pages 26 and 27. These pages contain directions for making some simple puppets and a stage. You may want your students to write their own puppet plays, or you may use one that is already in print (See the bibliography on page 48.)

Another early form of drama which is still popular is pantomime. The pantomime exercise on page 28 is ready to use as it is. Simply cut the strips apart and let students draw them from a hat. You could use a black bowler or a beret, similar to those pantomimists wear. Have students take turns performing their pantomimes on a day when you would like a quiet activity. Instead of drawing slips at random, you might prefer to leave the strips intact, make copies of the list, and allow students to choose their favorites. Students may brainstorm and come up with their own ideas. To expand, have students dress in costumes and white faces and videotape their performances. The video tapes could then be shown to other classes and/or at back-to-school night.

Reader's theater is a classic drama experience for students. Suggestions for *Reader's Theater* can be found on page 29. The suggestions are arranged in order from beginning reader's theater experiences to the more advanced.

Dialogue is an important component of drama. Students will have the opportunity to write their own dialogue on page 30. This will give them an opportunity to use prewriting tools and sharpen their listening and observational skills. When they perform their dialogues in class, they will receive feedback automatically about how smooth, realistic, and coherent their dialogues are.

Puppetry

Here are some easy puppets you can make!

Materials:

- old socks
- cardboard
- white glue
- newspaper
- rubber bands
- pieces of felt
- fabric scraps

- handkerchiefs, bandanas, scarves
- googly eyes
- markers, paint (tempera)
- cardboard tubes (from toilet paper and paper towels)
- scissors
- paper towels (plain white or tan colored)

You can make almost any kind of puppet from an old sock. Here's how to make a funny dragon:

1. Cut a circle about 4–6 inches (10–15 cm) in diameter out of cardboard and fold it in half.

2. Apply glue in a circle around the outer edge.

3. Push the circle into the sock, all the way to the end, with the glued edges facing the toe.

4. Push in the toe of the sock so it sticks to the glued circle and let dry. This will form the dragon's mouth.

5. Roll up two balls from newspaper, about one inch (2.54 cm) across, and push them into the heel of the sock. These will form the dragon's eyes.

6. Wrap rubber bands around the base of the newspaper balls to form eyes that stick up. Glue on googly eyes.

7. Cut felt scales and glue them on the dragon's back.

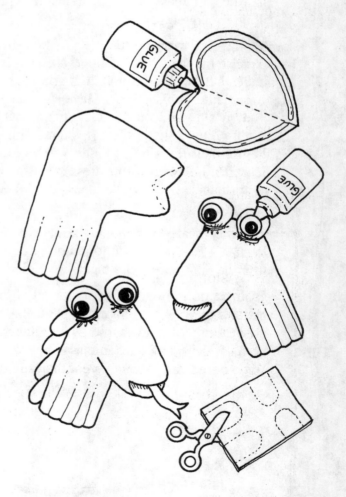

Puppetry *(cont.)*

Paper tubes are also good for making lots of different kinds of puppets. Here's how to make a wizard.

1. Cut a piece of cardboard tube about 2–3 inches (5–8 cm), depending on what you will make.

2. Tear a paper towel into pieces.

3. Mix together 3 tablespoons of white glue and 3 tablespoons of water.

4. Dip the paper towel pieces into the glue mixture and cover the outside of the tube with them.

5. Dip some more pieces of paper towel to make shapes like a nose and ears.

6. After it dries, use markers to draw the eyes, eyebrows, and mouth.

7. Out of cardboard, cut a cone-shaped hat, curl it into shape and tape it. Then glue it to the top of your wizard's head.

8. If you wish, you can decorate the hat with star stickers.

9. Drape a colorful handkerchief, bandana, or scarf over your hand. Put a rubber band around your little finger and the fabric and another rubber band around your thumb and the fabric. These will be the wizard's hands. Your middle three fingers, covered by fabric, go into the tube for the wizard's head.

To make a puppet stage:

1. Drape a sheet from a tabletop to the floor.

2. Puppeteers sit behind the table, hidden by the sheet.

3. Puppeteers raise hands to move puppets across the stage floor (tabletop).

4. Pin or attach stage decorations to the wall behind the table.

Once you have a set and some puppets, it's time to write a puppet play. Brainstorm for ideas and, if you want, you can outline your script by making Roman numeral I the beginning, II the middle, and III the end. Fill in the details of your outline and you'll have a basic script; you just need to add dialogue. Be sure to speak loudly and clearly when your puppet is speaking. You'll be hidden behind the stage so it will be harder to hear you. Also be sure to move your puppet when it is speaking.

At the library you will find books that tell how to make many more kinds of puppets and marionettes, too. Just about any story will make a good puppet show, but you can also find books in the library that have plays written especially for puppet presentation.

Pantomime

Pantomime is acting without speaking. All the information, the emotion, and the action have to be seen in your silent movements. When you pantomime, you must pay particular attention to your body motions and facial expressions. You might want to exaggerate your expressions, and you definitely want to have fun. Choose several ideas to pantomime from the following list.

◆ You are peeling onions.

◆ Your shoes are too tight.

◆ You ate much too much.

◆ You are washing a very large window.

◆ You are outside, and it is very hot.

◆ You are walking through mud.

◆ You see someone walk by, and you instantly fall in love.

◆ You feel a bug crawling down your back.

◆ You are going horseback riding for the first time.

◆ You are eating a very sour lemon.

◆ You just ate a large spoonful of peanut butter.

◆ You have a piece of cellophane stuck on your finger (and later stuck on your foot).

◆ You are walking across the room on a tightrope.

◆ You are chewing about six pieces of bubble gum.

◆ You are trying to start your motorcycle.

◆ You are just getting settled into your favorite chair after a hard day, and a fly lands on your nose.

◆ You are eating a watermelon on a hot day.

◆ You are making a snowman.

◆ You are at one end of the rope in a tug-of-war contest.

◆ You are in a small room with a skunk.

◆ You are sleeping and having a really good dream when your alarm goes off.

◆ You are sitting on a park bench enjoying your lunch when you realize that a snake is resting on the same bench.

◆ You are in-line skating through a crowd.

◆ You are the passenger in a car, and the driver is driving recklessly.

Work in groups of 2 to 3 students to list more pantomime activities to perform for the class.

Reader's Theater

To begin, use a simple story with plenty of dialogue. Have students sit in a circle or with their chairs facing one another. Each student needs a copy of the story. If possible, highlight a character's lines to make it easy for the reader.

As students become comfortable with the concept, add more things to do. Add a narrator, use a sound effects specialist, and have students add drama to their characterizations. Encourage them to practice until they find an appropriate voice for their character. Show them how to add emotion to their words.

There are many books and periodicals at the library which contain plays for young people and even plays specifically designed to be used for reader's theater. Finding a good one that is appropriate for your students will make all the difference. Then you will just need to make copies for your actors.

Most of the plays and reader's theater scripts that are available for young people are designed for classroom situations. You should feel free to modify any scripts, to add or remove a character, or to change some of the situations. If you want a play about space pioneers but can only find a play about covered wagon pioneers, for instance, you could modify the play from covered wagons to spacecraft and from prairies to moonscapes.

You might want to try a reader's theater play on stage. To do so, your main focus would be the words of the readers, the set (probably just some strategically placed chairs on the stage since the readers do not move around), and lighting. A reader's theater on stage can be just as dramatic as a regular play, even without elaborate sets, costumes and actions. It would be a good experience for your students to try a dramatic presentation that did not rely on the usual flash and special effects. Other classes could be invited to come and see the presentation.

Once your students have become accomplished reader's theater actors, they will be sure to want to try their hands at playwriting and directing. Divide them into teams and have them appoint playwrights, directors, actors, and set designers. Be sure they do prewriting activities. They might find the storyboard form (page 7) useful in the planning stages. An hour per week or per day, depending on your schedule, could be set aside for reader's theater teams to work on their productions.

When students are ready, they could present their work to other classes, have their presentations videotaped to be shown in a school film festival or for open house, and/or present a night of reader's theater to their parents.

Dramatic Dialogue

A dialogue is a conversation between two or more people. Dialogue is important in plays, novels, and in your life. Dialogue is all around you. Next time you are at a restaurant, or a market, or out anywhere, listen to conversations. You can tell a lot about people by the things they say and how they say them. When you write dialogue for a play or presentation, think about what you can say about a character and his or her situation through the things he or she says. Here are some dialogue exercises to try:

1. Listen to dialogue you hear somewhere in public. Write what you hear. Try writing what just one of the speakers said. What if the other speaker had said something different? Rewrite the dialogue of the other speaker so he or she is saying something completely different, but make it still respond to the first speaker's words.

2. Imagine some dialogue taking place. Write what just one of the speakers says. Trade papers with your classmates. Now each of you will fill in the missing dialogue. Take turns reading your dialogues out loud. How many of you were close to what was imagined?

3. No two writers are exactly the same. Fill in the missing dialogue below. When everyone is finished, read your work aloud. Notice how many different dialogues and situations you have created.

"I don't know."

_____

_____

"I said, 'I don't know'!"

_____

"Well, why should I?"

_____

"Look—if she doesn't care, why should I?"

_____

_____

"Well, if I go down there, I'll just stir up trouble—you know what I mean?"

_____

_____

"So what's next? I haven't a clue. Maybe if I hadn't said that thing . . . "

_____

_____

"Gimme a break! It was an honest mistake, like you've never made one!"

_____

_____

"That's right."

_____

_____

"I know, who would've ever thought it would turn out like that!"

_____

_____

4. Now break into teams to write a scene in which there is lots of dialogue. Some of you can be the actors and some the writers. Don't forget a director. You may also want a videographer. If you can videotape your presentation, hold a film festival in class. Or have a dialogue day and present your one-act dramas in class. Time your scene to be about five minutes long and be sure to leave your audience in suspense by writing drama that keeps them wondering what will be next. Your scene can conclude, or you can leave your audience hanging. You might want to add more scenes later.

Introduction

You may find it advantageous to carry over some of the activities from the last unit and use them in this unit, which focuses even more on drama. For instance, you will find an activity titled *Filmmaking* (page 32). Students will use storyboards to plan a five-minute movie with a plot and dialogue. If they need inspiration, they might want to use the scenarios from page 24 or a dialogue from the activity on page 30. If possible, you may have students work on their projects at school. If necessary, they may need to take turns with the video camera, so you may assign video days to the various teams. It might also be possible that students can team up after school and on weekends if they have access to video cameras. Some students may prefer to go on location to produce their films.

The *Slide Show* expands the skills of planning and creating a presentation. In this case there will be no dialogue, but students may wish to add music or tape-recorded narration. Students will create photographs, using transparency film, to present a story. They may write their own stories or choose a familiar story and have their friends pose as the characters. This activity reinforces editing and organizational skills. When the projects are completed, you may have students present them to the class. You will be able to handle several student presentations per day if they can arrange their slides in a loading tray or system that is compatible with the available slide projector. However, you may prefer to spread out the presentations over a longer period of time.

And Now a Word from Our Sponsor (page 34) is an activity which allows students to create their own commercials. The challenge to this activity is that the commercials will be only 60 seconds long. Students will learn to make every word count. Another challenge will be that students will need to create the commercial for a product that does not exist. They will need to brainstorm and create a product that they think ought to exist. You may wish to videotape their commercials. To expand this activity, incorporate student commercials into other student projects—for instance, *The Tongue Twisters Show* could be interrupted from time to time to bring viewers an "important message."

Finally, you will find in this section an activity for creating demonstrations. *How to Make a PBJ*, on page 35, directs students to create a "how-to" demonstration. Some students, depending upon their subject matter, may wish to teach a class with their audience participating in the learning process. Clarify with the students how they will be presenting their demonstrations before moving ahead with them. You may wish to videotape the demonstrations for the purposes of critique and/or to show to parents.

Filmmaking

You are now a filmmaker. Your job is to create a film that will entertain and delight your audience. Where to begin?

Meet with your team and brainstorm ideas. Your project will be a short film about five minutes long. You will need to write a short plot or scene, create characters, and determine what they will do and what they will say to each other. You may get ideas for a short skit or scene from library books. In the drama section you can find short plays, skits, and monologues. You may get an idea from other assignments you have had in class. Many ideas come from our own lives and experiences, so don't forget to look there too. You might even use William Shakespeare as a resource for ideas. Many playwrights and scriptwriters have borrowed from Shakespeare, why not you?

Next, decide who on your team will write your script, who will act in it, who will direct, and who will videotape it. Be sure to give credit to all those who worked on your film. You can use the storyboard form on page 7 to plan your film. You will probably need several pages of storyboards. Someone on your team can be the storyboard artist.

Next, make a shooting schedule. Everyone on your team will need a copy. Follow the schedule as you set up and videotape each scene. The director can call out "Take!" at the end of each successful scene, but don't relax until you see the "rushes" (recordings of the scenes you've shot). You may decide to do some of the scenes over again.

The director, or an assistant, will need to watch carefully to be sure the scene goes as planned and that there are no unexpected distractions, like a helicoptor overhead or a stray dog entering the scene.

Be sure to speak clearly in your scenes, and remember your audience will want to see action. Even if your scene calls for a simple conversation, move around and have the videographer choose different angles.

Don't forget to add music and graphics to your presentation. You can add recorded music in the background, or you might want to plan a skit that includes music in the plot if you have musicians or singers on your team. You can add graphics by splicing in a transparency to the videotape or creating graphics on posterboard to be videotaped. Include the title of your film and the credits.

When the director says "It's a wrap!", that means that you are finished filming. Next comes editing and promoting. And then, finally, your film will be released to be seen at a classroom near you, like your own. Don't be surprised if your film is seen in other classrooms and at back-to-school night. Be prepared to hear the reviews. You can count on some people not caring for your film and some loving it. Maybe if you prepare well, most people will love it.

Slide Show

They say a picture tells a thousand words. Photographers often say a great deal with their photographs. Sometimes they tell a story; sometimes they simply tell a great deal about their subject. This is your opportunity to express yourself as a photographic illustrator.

The first thing you will need to do is decide upon a story you want to tell. You may choose a favorite story, or you may wish to write your own. In either case, brainstorming will help you come up with ideas.

When you know what you want to do, plan it with a storyboard similar to the sample below. Each illustration will represent one slide. The tricky part will be adding music and narration. Once you have your narration written in the square next to its corresponding illustration, things should go smoothly.

Text Notes	Visual	Audio

Now go out and photograph. Be sure to use transparency film to get slides. Look at your storyboard to see what your picture will need to look like. If you are using your friends to play the characters, you will need to direct their poses and facial expressions.

Take more pictures than you will need because some of them are not going to come out as you expected.

When your film is processed, it is time to edit. Choose the best ones and put them in the proper order.

Next, you can add your narration and any sound. If you plan to speak while your slides are shown, write a script for yourself and number each section to match its corresponding slide. If you plan to tape record narration and music, you will need to play your slide show while you record the music and narration to be sure that everything matches up.

And Now a Word from Our Sponsor

Create and perform a 60-second commercial. Brainstorm until you come up with an idea for a product that does not exist but one that you wish existed or one that you think should exist.

Create a model of your product or use a large, poster-size drawing or photograph to illustrate your product.

Fill out the form below to plan your commercial. The word *copy* means the words that will be used in your commercial. In your copy be sure to include basic information about your product: why it is needed, the many uses of your product, and where it can be found, for example.

Be sure to be convincing. Your goal is to convince your viewers to want to run right out to buy your product. You can appeal to them by leading them to believe that with your product, they will be more "cool", more beautiful, more pleasant, safer, smarter, healthier, have more free time, or any other appealing reasons you can suggest.

The Product: _____

Actor or Actress: _____

Copy: _____

_____

_____

_____

_____

_____

_____

_____

_____

_____

Where it can be purchased: _____

_____

_____

_____

_____

How to Make a PBJ

Show the class how something is done or how it works. It could be as simple as how to make a peanut butter and jelly sandwich to as complicated as how a computer works. Don't skip any steps and be sure to add your own personal flair.   Keep the time of your speech between three and five minutes. Complete this page. Be sure to practice every step before you give your demonstration.

My topic: _____

Purpose: to show the class how to _____

Materials I need to bring for my demonstration: _____

_____

_____

_____

How will the class be able to see what I do? _____

_____

_____

Will I need anyone to help me?_____

Steps in my demonstration:

1. _____

2. _____

3. _____

4. _____

5. _____

6. _____

Introduction

Students need an opportunity, from time to time, to experience more exhuberant forms of language arts. This section begins with a show-and-tell activity with a twist: *Guess What!* (page 37). Because this activity also allows students to learn more each other, it would also be good as an introductory or icebreaking activity. You might prefer to use this show-and-tell activity as an ongoing part of the classroom program. If you wish, you could have students bring in their sacks on a designated date and keep them together. Then you could pull out one a day for show-and-tell.

Alphabet Games (page 38) strengthen oral skills and require quick thinking. These games will fit readily into any gaps in your schedule. Students may even decide to take these games home with them to play with their families. Alphabet games, of course, promote more than just fun (and often, hilarity!) with tongue twisting alliteration. These activities are powerful stimuli for vocabulary building; they direct attention to word choice, often producing surprising combinations of terms and turns of thought. Such wordplay develops linguistic agility and opens the students' minds to the real potential of language to stimulate thought. The real advantage is that all of this develops naturally, with pleasant associations of game playing.

Listen to This! (page 39) will introduce students to observational skills, technology skills, and editing skills as they search for and record unusual sounds. Also, some specific suggestions (or examples) in advance will help students get started and stimulate their own ideas. For example, try recording the sounds of a loose bicycle chain moving on its sprocket, the winding up of a mechanical alarm clock, a toaster as it pops up, a squeaky door, a skateboard rolling over a curb, a stone dropped in a shallow pan of water, etc. Urge the students to seek other, original, sounds from nature—wind through the leaves of a tree, water sounds from a fountain, or a branch rubbing against a window pane, for example. If you have especially rambunctious students, you may wish to issue guidelines or review the tapes the students bring in before playing them for the class.

I Totally Disagree! (pages 40–41) introduces students to persuasion, argument, and debate. Students will have a new way to look at arguments. They will learn how to support their point of view, a necessary skill for college and life. For the debate activity, appoint a moderator to time each team's argument time. Allot between one to three minutes for each team's turns. Allow two to four turns per team per topic. On page 40 you will find some debate topics. These may be cut out and distributed to the teams. As always, they are only a springboard to inspire you. Modify topics to suit your needs and add more. For instance, you may prefer to have topics that reinforce what is being taught in social studies.

Guess What!

Want to keep your classmates guessing? Here's what you do.

- ◆ Go home and find something that would represent you. For instance, if you love to play ice hockey, choose a hockey puck. If you love art, choose a watercolor that you painted. If you collect something, choose an item from your collection.

- ◆ Put the item in a brown lunch bag or grocery bag.

- ◆ On a piece of paper write about the item. For instance, if you love horseback riding, you might write: "I love to go horseback riding. I started taking lessons when I was three years old. Now I compete in equestrian events. I won a blue ribbon this year. My name is Nickie G." Put this inside the bag along with a horseshoe.

- ◆ Next, write three clues about what is in the bag. For instance, if you put a horse shoe in the bag, your clues might be: "It is shaped like the letter C," "It is made of metal," "It is footwear."

- ◆ Write your clues on separate pieces of paper and put them in an envelope. Seal the envelope.

- ◆ Staple the bag closed, and staple the envelope to the top of the bag.

- ◆ Bring your bag to school on the day your teacher has told you it is due.

Your teacher will collect all the bags for show and tell.

When your teacher gets to your bag, he or she will read one clue at a time and allow your classmates to try to guess what is in the bag.

Once your item is revealed, your teacher will read what you had to say about horseback riding, but she won't reveal your name until your classmates have had a chance to try to guess who brought the horseshoe for show and tell.

Alphabet Games

Alphabet Sentences

To play this game, students sit in a circle. It can be played with just two students or up to a class if all can hear. The first student to play has the letter "A." He or she must create a sentence using as many words that start with the letter "A" as possible. Conjunctions and one preposition are free, and they get one more free word. Subtract one point each for any additional words that do not start with the assigned letter. Sentences may not consist of just one word. As soon as the student can no longer continue, he or she must stop, and a scorekeeper will keep track of the final score. Players get five points for each word that begins with the assigned letter. The next player gets the letter "B" and the next the letter "C," and so on. If a player gets an especially difficult letter like "X," he or she may choose to try to get some points or skip a turn. The next player would go on with the next letter. If played in small groups, players who skip a turn are more likely to be able to catch up on their next turn. Here is a sample sentence: "Attractive and artistic, Amanda Ann Andersen ate anchovies, asparagus, and artichokes at an Anchorage, Alaska academy and asked Andy Archibald for another aspirin." (110 points)

Alphabet Families

To play, students sit in a circle and present fictional family information in alphabetical order. Each family must include the father's and mother's first and last names, the occupations of the parents, the street name where they live, the town they live in, and the names of at least two children. If a player is unable to give all the information in the given time (set a timer for 30 seconds to two minutes for beginners), he or she must drop out until the next round. Here is a sample family:

> *Bernie and Beatrice Baumwagen, Bernie is a bus driver, Beatrice is a beautician, they live on Bronco Buster Blvd. in Boston, and their children's names are Barrie, Bennie, Bonnie and Bunnie.*

I'm Going to . . .

This is played the same as above but the first says, "I am Abigail Alvarez and I am taking an airplane to Africa and I am bringing answering machines," because she is assigned the letter "A." The next student says something like, "I am Benjamin Barker, and I am taking a plane to Beirut, and I am bringing baby buggies." Each student fills in a name slot, a location slot, and an object slot with his or her assigned alphabet letter.

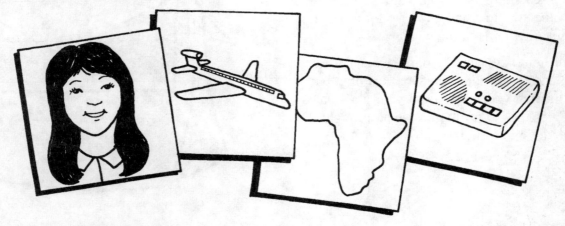

Listen to This! Sound Effects Collection

Stop and close your eyes. What do you hear? Sometimes when we pay attention, we hear sounds we didn't even know were there. This is your chance to really listen and to let others listen to what you heard. Here's what you do:

◆ Acquire a tape recorder and blank tape.

◆ Wander about and listen for sounds that you may not have noticed before. Some sounds might be so familiar to you that you might want to tape them just to see what they sound like after being taped. You might be surprised to discover that they sound different when taped.

◆ Try to find sounds that will stump your classmates.

◆ Make a collection of about five minutes of different sounds. Try to have at least four to five different sounds. Leave some silent time on the tape between recorded sections to have a clear separation of sounds.

◆ Bring them to school.

◆ When your teacher says it's your turn, you will play your tape and see if anyone can guess what the sounds are.

◆ Listen carefully to the tapes of others. See if you can guess what they taped.

Did anyone tape the same sounds?

When you make your tape, fill in the form below, but don't let anyone else see it until after they hear your tape and make their guesses.

Sound #1: _____   Sound #5: _____

Recorded at: _____   Recorded at: _____

Sound #2: _____   Sound #6: _____

Recorded at: _____   Recorded at: _____

Sound #3: _____   Sound #7: _____

Recorded at: _____   Recorded at: _____

Sound #4: _____   Sound #8: _____

Recorded at: _____   Recorded at: _____

I Totally Disagree!

To argue effectively you need to prove your point with support. Support is the same thing as evidence, proof, or convincing facts to make your point. To practice supporting your point of view, fill in the following with three supporting ideas each:

1. Why I like to laugh:_____

_____

_____

2. Why I like holidays: _____

_____

_____

3. Why I like candy: _____

_____

_____

4. Why I like music: _____

_____

_____

Now try completing the following sentences with three descriptions:

1. Yardwork is_____

_____

2. Gum is _____

_____

3. Homework is_____

_____

Now pick a topic and plan to persuade your classmates. Fill in the form below and use it as your notes for a two- to three-minute persuasive speech.

My topic: _____

I will persuade the class that: _____

This topic is important to me because: _____

Three supporting facts about my topic: _____

_____

Three supporting examples about my topic: _____

_____

My personal opinion about the topic:_____

I Totally Disagree! *(cont.)*

Now that you have learned how to support your points, you are ready to debate. When you debate, you will be on a team arguing for your opinion while another team opposes you. When your teacher has everyone assigned to teams of three to four students each, you will be given a debate topic. Don't be surprised if your topic is silly or something that you don't agree with. The point is to learn to support your topic with reasonable arguments. You will be given time to prepare for your debate. This would be a good time to look up facts in references and computer encyclopedias.

When the debate is presented, you will be given time for one of your team members to present the topic and your position. Then the opposing team will be given the same opportunity. Be sure to listen carefully. You might want to take notes on what the opposing team says. When it is your turn again, you will want to argue against things that the other team said and support your argument with evidence, facts, and proof. When it is their turn, they will do the same. Your teacher will tell you how much time you will be given, and a moderator will be appointed to let you know when your turn is over.

Debate Topics

Team #1

- The earth is flat.
- A woman would make a good president.
- School uniforms are a bad idea.
- Junk food should be outlawed.
- Elephants make good pets.
- School should be in session for just three months per year.
- Spiders are wonderful.
- Watching television is a waste of time.
- There are definitely extraterrestrial beings.
- The best place for a vacation is the beach.
- Exercise is important.
- Dogs need sweaters in the winter.
- Books are better than movies.

Team #2

- The earth is round.
- A woman would not make a good president.
- School uniforms are a good idea.
- Junk food is beneficial.
- Elephants make terrible pets.
- School should be in session for eleven months per year.
- Spiders are disgusting.
- Watching television is a good idea.
- There's no such thing as extraterrestrials.
- The best place for a vacation is the mountains.
- Exercise is a waste of time.
- Dogs don't ever need to wear clothes.
- Movies are better than books.

Introduction

The activities in this section introduce students to the amazing world of multimedia. Multimedia allows students various options for presenting information and expressing themselves. Students with various capabilities and intelligences can learn to create presentations that utilize their own capacities to the maximum extent.

The use of multimedia will strengthen the students' skills in researching, writing, organizing, critical thinking, problem solving, and relating and applying ideas.

The section begins with instruction in the use of HyperStudio® (pages 44 and 45). Other multimedia programs will be similar, but in any case, the literature and tutorials that accompany the software should be referred to for more information. The directions can be copied and used as a reference or a tutorial. Keep in mind, however, that reading about how to use multimedia can be overwhelming and possibly confusing at first. You might prefer to simply load the program and begin to experiment. This is one time when it might be better to leave the directions for later. HyperStudio is user-friendly, and one can learn to create a stack without looking at a manual. After everyone has had an opportunity to explore the program, the instructions might be even more helpful.

After students have gained confidence with multimedia, they will create a book report or research report (pages 46 and 47) using HyperStudio. They will find the *Hyperstack Planning Form* (page 43) to be useful, and it will allow you to determine at a glance their readiness to go on to the actual computer work. You may choose to have your students do only the book report, only the research report, or both. The book report would be good as an introduction since the subject won't require much additional research. For the research report, give your students a list of subjects. You may coordinate the research topic with your curriculum or create a list appropriate to the abilities of your students. You will also want to let them know how many cards you expect for their multimedia report.

The practice in producing this multimedia presentation will prove invaluable to the students in your class. Providing such activities means that your are arming students with a package of skills that will serve them well in all other subjects in school and prepare them for the now necessary requirements of the business world. Students familiar with the technology of multimedia and skilled in its use are gaining the necessary equipment to become the competent citizens of tomorrow, productive members of our society. The results will produce a clear and evident sense of accomplishment for the students and the teacher.

Hyperstack Planning Form

Use the form below to plan your HyperStudio, or other multimedia, presentation. Be sure to include the placement of buttons, graphics, and text.

Create a Multimedia Presentation

Getting started

1. Once you have opened HyperStudio, click the "New Stack" icon.
2. Choose "Save As" from the "File" menu, name your file, and save it.
3. Choose the "Tools" menu and click and hold the mouse button down while you drag it off to the side. Do the same with the "Colors" menu.

Creating the Cards

Background

1. Choose "Import Background" from the "File" menu.
2. Locate the HS Art folder, which is in the HyperStudio folder.
3. Locate Dingbats 1, Dingbats 2, Computer 1, or Computer 2 and open one of them.
4. Click on the "Selection" tool from the toolbox. Select everything in the picture except the border. Press the delete key.

Title

1. Choose "Add a Text Object" from the "Objects" menu.
2. When the box appears, click outside of the box.
3. Then, on the screen that appears, click "Style." You will need to choose a point size, font, and color for your title.
4. Choose "Center" where it says "Align," and then click off the Xs where it says, "Scrollable" and "Draw Scroll Bar." Click "OK."
5. Give your stack a title that includes your name, and save your work.

Clip Art

1. Choose "Clip Art" from the "File" menu.
2. Locate the HS Art folder, choose one of the art cards in the folder, and open it.
3. When you have the picture you want, select the lasso tool and circle the part of the picture you want, and then click "OK."

   Note: If the first card you choose does not have a picture you want, click on "Get another picture."
4. When you find a picture you want, repeat step 3.
5. When the picture you choose appears on the screen, use the mouse and drag it to where you want it on the screen.

The Button

1. Choose "Add a Button" from the "Objects" menu.
2. You now have several choices to make. You can make the text and background of your button match the color of your stack. You also need to put some text on your button so anyone looking at your stack will know how the button should be used. For instance, "Next Card" can be typed in the name box.
3. When selecting your button shape, choose only from the top four button shapes on the top left corner of the dialogue box.
4. After you have chosen a button shape, click on "Icons" and choose an icon to go inside your button. Be sure all three boxes have Xs on the bottom left of the dialogue box. Click "OK."

Create a Multimedia Presentation *(cont.)*

The Button *(cont.)*

5. When the button appears on your card, use the mouse to drag it to where you want it and then click outside of the button to place it.

6. After placing your button, the "Actions" dialogue box will appear. Then on the left side of the box, under "Places to Go," choose "Another Card." When the next box comes up, choose the left or right arrow and click "OK."

7. Finally, select a transition. Click on "Try It" before clicking "OK." If you like it, click "OK."

8. To begin the next card in your stack, choose "New Card" from the "Edit" menu.

Additional Ideas for Cards

To Animate

1. Use a pencil tool or a paintbrush tool from the toolbox to draw a picture to animate. Use the paint bucket tool to fill your picture with the color you choose.

2. To animate, choose "Add a Button" from the "Objects" menu. Choose the button color and put text on the button (for example, "Animate 1"). Choose button shape.

3. Drag the button into place with the mouse, click outside of the button and the "Actions" dialogue box will appear. Under "Things to Do," choose "New Button Actions."

4. When the "New Button Actions" dialogue box appears, click on "Animator," and then click on "Use This NBA."

5. When the next screen appears, click on the lasso, and then click on "From the Screen." Lasso the entire picture or the part of the picture you want to move. Move the picture where you want it and then click the mouse.

6. When the dialogue box comes back, click on "Hide Background" on the first frame and click "OK" twice. Try out your new button!

To Add Text

1. Choose "Add a Text Object" from the "Objects" menu. When the text box appears, click outside it, and that will cause the "Text Appearances" dialogue box to appear.

2. Choose "Style" When the next box appears, select a font, point size, and a color. Click "OK."

3. Type your text. If you want the scroll bar to appear, fill the text box. Then you can add a scrolling button by choosing "Add a Button" from the "Objects" menu.

4. Choose your colors and text for your button ("Scroll").

5. Next you will need to choose your "New Button Actions" ("Roll Credits") and choose a scrolling speed.

The Last Button

1. Follow the directions above to choose colors, icon, text, and background for your button. Your last button will be named "Beginning," "Home," or possibly, "Table of Contents."

2. Experiment with HyperStudio. You can go back into your cards and add more clip art. You can add sound to a button. You can paint the background a different color. You can get graphics from The Writing Center of the Scrapbook. Try different things and explore. It's easy to start over if you don't like the results.

Create a Multimedia Book Report or Research Report

Now that you have practiced using multimedia, here is your opportunity to create a report. You will be able to make your report "come alive" with the advantages of multimedia.

Create your first card as a title page and home page. On this card you will want to include the title of the book or your report, the author's name, and your name. Also include any graphics you want. Add buttons to direct viewers to the other cards in your stack. For instance, if your book report is on *Little House on the Prairie*, you might want a button labeled "About the Author" to lead to a card about Laura Ingalls Wilder. You might also want to include any of the following buttons: "Other Books by Laura Ingalls Wilder," "Prairie Life," "Excerpts from the Book," and/or "What I Like About the Book." If someone were to click on the "About the Author" button, he or she might find something like the following: a photograph of Laura Ingalls Wilder, a scrollable biography, background art of her environment, and perhaps a video clip of the author speaking. There might be a segment from the television series depicting Laura or possibly an audio clip of music from the television program. Also, on this card, you will need a "Home" button so that persons exploring your hyperstack can go back to the first card (the title/home card). Then they can click on another button to explore further.

When you create a multimedia research report, choosing a topic may be the most difficult part even when your teacher gives you guidelines. Pick a topic that will really shine with multimedia. For instance, if you were to pick the topic of Martin Luther King, Jr., you would find quotations, photographs, video clips, and biographical information. You would also find a great deal of related material on the civil rights movement, Black history, nonviolent civil disobedience, prejudice, and slavery.

Begin by planning what information you will include. An outline would be a good idea, but you may use whatever organizational form you prefer. Using notecards to collect information works especially well with multimedia because you will be creating cards on the computer. Arrange the cards according to topic, and then when you have collected and organized your information, use the notecards to plan each hyperstack card. You may prefer to use the Hyperstack planning form on page 43

Create a Multimedia Book Report or Research Report *(cont.)*

Once you have a plan in place, it will be time to create the first card in your stack. Your teacher will tell you how many cards are expected, so plan accordingly.

As with other Hyperstudio presentations, consider your first card to be the cover of your report. For this report, you can put the title on this card, your name, art, and just one button. Your button may be titled "Click here" or "Contents."

Your second card will be your table of contents. You will need to decide whether you want viewers of your report to go through each card in sequence or if you want them to be able to choose where they want to go and be able then to return to the contents. Usually you will want them to be able to do the latter. It is more fun and more interesting to be able to explore. Assign a button for each section of your report and don't forget a button to get back to the cover so viewers can exit when finished. You can title it "exit". If there is room, you can add graphics and a video clip.

The rest of your cards will be dedicated to your subtopics. For instance, you might have a card that is listed in the table of contents as "Quotations." When that button is clicked on, the "Quotations" card will appear. If your report is on Martin Luther King, Jr., you could have, on this card, scrollable text of the "I Have a Dream" speech. You might have a quotation across the card as background, along with a photograph or drawing of King. You would definitely want a video clip of Martin Luther King, Jr., delivering a speech. There are many options and it will be up to you. Be sure to include on each card a button that will take the viewer back to the table of contents. The button can be labeled, "Table of Contents," "Contents," "Back," "Exit," or whatever will indicate that clicking that button will lead back to the beginning.

For your final card, you will create a bibliography. This is a time when you will take full advantage of the scroll bar. You will be able to put an entire bibliography in a window which the viewer can scroll. That will leave room on your final page for some more art or a final video, if you like. You might also want to use this page to give credit for any photographs or videos you used. If you have a list, you might want to put the credits in another window with a scroll bar. Be sure to include on your final page a button that will lead back to the table of contents or title page. You don't want your viewers to get stuck on your last page. You want them to be able to go back and take another look at an interesting page.

When you have completed a multimedia report, congratulate yourself. You have really accomplished something! Now you can really say, "I can give a presentation!"

Resources

Books

Arnold, Arnold. *The Big Book of Tongue Twisters and Double Talk*. Random House, 1964.

Borman, Jaime Lynee. *Computer Dictionary for Kids: . . . and Their Parents*. Barron's Educational Series, Inc., 1995.

Bryant, Mary Helen. *Integrating Technology into the Curriculum*. Teacher Created Materials, Inc., 1996.

Creegan, George. *Sir George's Book of Hand Puppetry*. Follett Publishing Company, 1966.

Dana, Ann, Marianne Handler, and Jane Peters Moore. *Hypermedia as a Student Tool: A Guide for Teachers*. Teacher Ideas Press, 1995.

Dunbar, Robert E. *How to Debate*. Franklin Watts, 1987.

Fontaine, Robert. *Humorous Skits for Young People*. Plays, Inc., 1970.

Gilfond, Henry. *How to Give a Speech*. Franklin Watts, 1980.

Hayes, Deborah Shepherd. *Managing Technology in the Classroom*. Teacher Created Materials, Inc., 1995.

Hayes, Deborah Shepherd. *Multimedia Projects*. Teacher Created Materials, Inc., 1997.

LeBaron, John and Philip Miller. *Portable Video*: *A Production Guide for Young People*. Prentice-Hall, Inc., 1982.

Mandell, Muriel. *Games to Learn By*. Sterling Publishing Co., Inc., (Oak Tree Press Co., Ltd., London & Sydney), 1973.

McBride, Karen Hein and Elizabeth DeBoer Luntz. *Help! I Have Hyperstudio...Now What Do I Do?* McB Media, 1996

Miller, Helen Louise. *First Plays for Children*. Plays, Inc., 1971.

Pereira, Linda. *Computers Don't Byte*. Teacher Created Materials, Inc., 1996.

Philpott, A.R., ed. *Eight Plays for Hand Puppets*. Plays, Inc., 1972.

Seto, Judith Roberts. *The Young Actors Workbook*. Grove Press, Inc., 1979.

Supraner, Robyn and Lauren Supraner. *Plenty of Puppets to Make*. Troll Associates, 1981.

Wallace, Mary. *I Can Make Puppets*. Owl Books, 1994.

Wodaski, Ron. *Absolute Beginner's Guide to Multimedia*. Sams Publishing, 1994.

Yerian, Cameron and Margaret, ed. *Fun Time Plays and Special Effects*. Children's Press, 1975.

Software

HyperStudio 3.0. Roger Wagner Publishing, Inc., 1050 Pioneer Way, Suite P., El Cajon, California 92020. 1-800-421-6526.

Kid Pix 2. Broderbund Software Direct, P.O. Box 6125, Novato, CA 94948-6125. 1-800-474-8840.

Multimedia Workshop. Davidson and Associates, 19840 Pioneer Ave., Torrance, CA 90503. 1-800-545-7677.